Donald's   ͻ

A brief resume of the life of
Captain Donald E. Baines

Written by Donald E. Baines
(with the assistance of various people)

Published in 2021 by Vantage Publishing Limited
9 Chestnut Suite, Guardian House, Godalming, Surrey GU7 2AE
www.vantagepublishing.co.uk

ISBN: 978-1-8383469-2-8

AUTHORS NOTE

Having been diagnosed with the onset of Alzheimers a few years ago it was a distressing thought to realise what this disease held for me for the future.

In looking at all my old naval and airline logbooks which I have kept throughout the whole of my professional life, together with various items of correspondence received in thanks for airline related events, I found myself wondering how long it might be before these items no longer had relevance for me.

Flying for me has been a love, and a true passion, since the start of my career and even since having to give it up due to medical issues my love for it has never faltered.

In an attempt to keep my brain active, I decided to write "Donald's Story" and put down on paper all the memories that I still was able to recall and which I very much cherish. In doing so I have found that by giving myself this challenge my long-term memory has improved albeit sometimes having difficulty with the time frames.

I hope "Donald's Story" is as interesting for you to read as it will be for me as a reminder of the most fortunate life I have lived.

Donald Edmund Baines

DONALD'S STORY

List of the Aircrafts flown in both the Navy and as a Commercial Pilot with British European Airways and British Airways

Various Photographs and Letters

Chapter 1 : IN THE BEGINNING

Some of the best stories start with "in the beginning…….." and so I shall start mine …… in the beginning.

I was born on March 5th in 1935, the youngest child of Philip and Eileen Baines, with a brother Ralph, elder by 3 years and a sister Sheila, who was only 1 year older than me.

My mother Eileen (nee McDonald) came from Wallasey, Wirral, Cheshire. She had gone to the Liverpool School of Art and was a brilliant artist who had many of her own exhibitions. She was a warm, loving mother, a lively person who was always good fun.

My father who came from Rock Ferry in Cheshire was second in charge as a Cotton Broker working for the George Bridge Company in Liverpool. When the second world war began and they started advertising for men to join the army, he decided to sign up at the age of 36. He was placed with the tank regiment and when they were in Tobruk, Lybia, North Africa and under attack the tracks of his tank were blown off so they could not move and they had to bail out through the bottom hatch on the floor of the tank. The two soldiers at the top of the tank died. My father and another soldier managed to pull themselves out, however my father had lost one of his legs below the knee and the other soldier had lost his eye and an arm. They treated him, as best as was possible at the field hospital and then when he was stable, he was transferred to a bigger military hospital where they had to amputate another 2 inches from his leg. I recall him telling us his memory of hearing the doctor say, "pass the saw nurse", which was a handsaw, then he fortunately passed out having been given the gas anaesthetic.

Once he was able to travel, they transported him to Baragwaneth Hospital, Johannesburg, South Africa. After several months recovering, they transported him, by road, to Durban, South Africa,

3

and then to a troop ship at the Durban docks. From there they travelled on the troop ship all the way around Africa back to the UK, avoiding the Mediterranean and the German U-boats.

The family at that time lived in Eastham village, near Ellesmere Port, which was near the start of the Manchester Ship Canal. This is where the ships bringing supplies into Manchester became a target for bombings during the war. Our home wasn't far from the Hooton Park RAF Airfield. This was only for a short time, about six months, and then we moved about three miles away, in 1936, to "Burford", Briardale Road, just off Mill Lane in Willaston Village. The new house was a large four bedroomed home, which had a separate garage and outbuildings that included a coal house, washroom and a toilet, with a large garden all around the property.

Willaston was a large village on the Wirral Peninsula in Cheshire, which was in the region of the RAF Hooton anti-submarine base. Here they had the Anson two-seater, twin engine, light aircraft which could attack ships with depth charges and keep a look out for enemy aircraft and boats, including submarines. These Anson aircraft flew over our home every 10 minutes or so. It seems that the air and the sea played a part in my life even before I knew it.

I have very fond memories of my childhood and clearly in my mind are memories of my father preparing the house in readiness for the war and the bombings that were to come. My father had the wash-house roof reinforced with concrete and equipped it with bunk beds and a separate escape door, this became our air-raid shelter during the war where we spent a considerable amount of time as the area around where we lived was heavily bombed. Although I was only the age of 4 when the war broke out, I can remember the many nights spent sleeping in the bunks in the washhouse. My father also had built, what he called a "bomb blast" wall, about 7 feet high. This was 4 feet away from the washhouse, the flat roof of which he had reinforced with concrete.

As far as education goes, I went to the private school of Summer Fields at Ledsham near Little Sutton. I recall my mother driving me to school with a great pal of mine, Chris Kenrick, in our Morris 10 green car. My brother and sister had to cycle down to Hooton Station to catch the steam train to Birkenhead and Chester as Ralph attended St Anselms, Birkenhead and Sheila attended Urseline Convent, Chester. At the age of 7, I joined my brother at the prep-school of St Anselms, Birkenhead which was run by the Catholic Christian Brothers who were mainly Irish.

I would walk from home to the Hadlow Road station in Willaston, which was about a mile away. From there I took a Great Western Railway train to Hooten. The train came from West Kirby to Hooton and then carried on to Wood Side Station at Birkenhead. Quite a journey for a young chap to travel on his own. My brother Ralph did join me for part of the journey. I was too young to cycle but he had to cycle with my sister down to Hooton station, where my sister went on to Chester, while Ralph and I continued the journey together, on an "LMS Steam" train. I remember the journey took us through the tunnel but not to Liverpool, it took a turning in the tunnel to Birkenhead. From the station we then had to catch a bus to our school. I will always remember the journey cost 2 old pence each way.

At the age of 11 (1946) my schooling carried on at Mount St Mary's College, a Jesuit boarding school on the Derbyshire/Nottinghamshire/South Yorkshire border, where Ralph was already attending. In fact, it was a school that my father and his brothers had attended, years before.

I recall the school laid on special carriages attached to mainline trains for its pupils when travelling to and from school. I travelled from Liverpool and a Master of the school would always be present in the carriages to check safe arrival/departures of pupils. The train went to Manchester and then onto Sheffield.

One often reads of people recalling horrendous times at boarding school, but my memories are of great happy times. I loved the school and enjoyed all the opportunities it gave me. I did extremely well in the subjects of Geography, French, Science and Physics, although I found the Latin and Greek, which we had to learn, hard work as they were new subjects for me.

It was at this time that I realised the importance of my Catholic faith and diligently undertook my duties as acolyte helping the priest during school services, which were in Latin. Later in life I was to perform the same duties at my local church and the strength of my faith has carried me through many a challenging time.

The school gave me the opportunity to expand my love of sport. I was a member of the under 14's rugby team before I eventually became a member of the 1st 15 rugby team. I was also in charge of the gymnastic team and was a keen tennis player. Cricket however was not for me, I considered it a boring game which did not interest me.

I worked hard at school and was rewarded with good grades in the General Certificate of Education, passing 7 Subjects. Leaving school at the age of 17, I had in my mind to follow in my father's footsteps and become a cotton broker, but the industry had been nationalised and he advised me that there was no future there.

One day my father showed me a newspaper advertisement from the Liverpool Daily Post, which was asking the question "why not learn to fly in the Navy and do your 2 years National Service in the Royal Naval Air Service?" (the name was later changed back to Fleet Air Arms). He thought this would be a good career for me and suggested I make contact and follow it up, which I did. I telephoned and was sent an application form, which I completed giving my schooling achievements and my sporting interests. I was contacted and asked to confirm my age and date of birth. When asked when I would like to start, I answered "as soon as possible" as I was only doing odd jobs for my father to fill in time. I was told that they wanted people like me, so I joined up at the age of 17 and a half, in 1952.

Chapter 2 : ON THE SEA AND IN THE AIR

I started my 2 years National Service in 1952 and was sent down to Lea-on-Solent, near Portsmouth. We were taken to a naval training base, for a 3-week course, at HMS Daedalus. This course was an initiation and introduction and included all medical check up's etc. We were then taken by boat across the water to the HMS Indefatigable training carrier, which had no aircraft on board. The lower deck had been converted into classrooms. Nearby there was also a 2nd Training aircraft carrier, also converted into classrooms called HMS Implacable which later joined us at a different mooring in Gibraltar harbour.

After the 3 weeks training I went on the ship HMS Indefatigable, out to Gibraltar for 3 months training. En-route training included learning how to transfer a man from a destroyer across to another ship by rope/wire, a system called a "Jackstay Transfer". Another example of the training was learning about the 3 different types of ships and how they all operate.

During our time in Gibraltar we were only allowed off the ship at weekends. The ship being docked at what was known as a "Mole", a massive structure of stone with a building on top used as a pier. Being a keen runner, I joined the running club which ran most days and I regularly ran from one Mole to another and then through the tunnel from one side of the island to the other, east to west and back.

The 3 months training was hard work, but I enjoyed it, even managing to sleep in a hammock which we rigged up every night and stowed vertically in daytime. I recall the Chief Petty Officer, named Clayton, who was our instructor, stressed to us, "that the first important step was to become a Naval Officer and that the Navy must always come first, the flying comes afterwards".

After training for 3 months, I went out to sea on a Minelayer for an exercise to see some air-to-air firing. This was with big guns no.

7.2 inches of high velocity, used to shoot aircraft down. An aircraft would fly alongside the ship at a certain distance away pulling what was known as a "drogue", a big, perforated sheet. The ship would be manoeuvred into the correct position and then the shells, which were painted were fired. These exercises were carried out at high speed in rough waters. I recall the Chief Petty Officer painting the shells with differing colours to differentiate the distances they had been fired from. Even in the most turbulent of waters he positioned himself to keep a steady hand; we trainees held on for our lives!

As Mid shipmen we were required to keep a journal and write in it every day journaling our activities and experiences. I still have mine to this day. On one aircraft carrier we had a Chief Officer named Colman, a member of the Colman Mustard family, who was married to a member of the Royal Family. He was in charge of sports and often took chaps to the London Boat Race because he used to be a rowing man. Unfortunately, I was never included, rowing being a sport that I had never got involved with.

I recall him asking me one day "are you enjoying your service Baines?" My answer being "yes, very hard work but enjoyable". He went on to correct me when I spoke about propellers hanging on "walls" in the school room, by pointing out that they were not walls, they were bulkheads. "Remember that" he told me, and I have.

After this training we sailed back to Portland Harbour near Weymouth where I was given a travel voucher and allowed to journey home for a few days. However, before this, I had to attend a review of my training with the Captain in the Quarter Deck of the Carrier. I had to walk through the Officers Wardroom, which was normally prohibited to the junior ranks. The Captain said, "Mr Baines have you enjoyed your experience?" and I responded that I had loved it. He then asked me which way the wind was blowing. Easterly I replied. "How do you know?" he asked. I informed him that I lived on the Wirral peninsula, which lay between the river Dee and the river Mersey, in a house that faced North, East, South and West, that I had experienced North Westerly winds from over the Mersey, South Westerly prevailing quite wet and showery weather, Southerly winds mainly calm due to high pressure and Easterly very strong, violent gales and usually unpleasant weather. I told him I had always been interested in meteorology and had very much enjoyed the courses we had taken.

Then he said "it is my job and my pleasure to promote you to become Midshipman in His Majesty's navy." This was the lowest "officer" position. Then he said "you may stand up and salute me", which I did, and then he told me to stay where I was and he stood up and he saluted me, something which was unheard of. He then said that I had done extremely well and come out top of the class. I was absolutely delighted and quite proud to have achieved this at the age of 18. He said that once you have said goodbye to your friends, I would like to talk to you so please come back and see me. On returning he told me that he had something very serious to say to me. He said all the reports he had from my other officers agreed with him and he said "you are extremely suitable to be offered a Long-Term Commission in Her Majesties Navy. You will have wonderful prospects on the new ships coming out. The decision is yours and you can always come back to the Navy for a long-term commission". I felt flattered and honoured.

After my short break at home, I was stationed at the Naval Airbase in Gosport where I was to attend a 3-month course at the pre-flight training school at HMS Siskin. Initially the training was all schoolroom based with studies covering such topics as aircraft engines, air frames, air law, airmanship, and metrology.

It wasn't all work however and I had the opportunity of improving my tennis when I joined the Alverstoke tennis club where I spent many an hour on the courts.

My first time on board an aircraft, a twin seater called a Sea Baliol, was when an Instructor took me on a flight over the airfield and the surrounding area. I was thrilled and absolutely loved the experience. It was wonderful to see from the air areas that previously I had only seen from on the ground and from looking at maps when studying them, especially the Naval Ships on the Solent and the Passenger Liners at Southampton Docks. The flight which lasted about 45 minutes was aimed at encouraging us, and I have to say I was totally enthralled by the experience. I instantly knew that flying was for me and that I was going to work hard to achieve my goal.

Our training continued on the ground and we were introduced to the 'Ejector Seat' and how to wear the parachute. There were various exercises to master, one I recall being the practice of how to get out of a Seafire 17 which was the equivalent of a Spitfire 22. When in the aircraft, on the ground, they had the engine running and the propellers turning, this to give a true to life feeling and for us to know what to expect by experiencing how the air flowed from the propeller which was the equivalent of the air flow in the air.

The three months for me passed very quickly and although I had thoroughly enjoyed my time at Gosport, I was keen to move on to the next stage of my training which would take me into the air.

Chapter 3 : THE THRILL OF LEARNING TO FLY

On departing Gosport, I was given leave and instead of heading back home to Cheshire I took the opportunity of visiting a friend, called Glen Gross, who was living in Barnet, North London.

From London I made my way to the RAF Syerston Base at Newark, Nottinghamshire, a large facility with Officer's Quarters and an Officer's Mess which was called "the Wardroom". The accommodation was individual rooms, although a few were shared, and we had the services of a "batman", this is a naval name for a steward. A new experience for me.

Our training was split between morning and afternoon sessions. One studying in the classroom and the other up in the air, learning to fly the aircraft. Our group was split into two. One group in the classroom for a morning and the other in the air, then in the afternoon the groups swapped activities.

On my morning flying sessions I was always early, helping to push the light training aircrafts out of the hanger. We trained on the Percival Prentice plane which was a basic trainer for the RAF. It was a low-wing monoplane with a fixed tailwheel undercarriage. The front seating was in a side-by-side configuration with a rear seat provided. It has a wingspan of 14 meters.

The other plane used in training was a De Havilland with a Gypsy Queen engine, which was a six-cylinder aero engine of 9.2 litre capacity.

The training period at Syerston, was Monday to Friday for 9 months, during which time I was taught all the aspects of the flying that I needed to know. I was given the opportunity of putting what was taught into practice, I went SOLO doing circuits around the airfield, various landing practices and training on speeds. I recall the instructions given to me by one instructor who said "at 10 to 12 feet above the ground when coming into land, take the power off and glide down easing back on the stick. Nose too high and you will be in trouble". However, I performed the task correctly, and was complimented with the remark. "Very nice landing Baines".

Whilst at Syerston, I bought myself a BSA 250cc motorbike, for the then vast sum of £45. I was very pleased indeed when I passed my test the first time of taking it, at Newark, a nearby village. This bike gave me the freedom to travel home to Cheshire at the weekends, not only to see my family but also my first girlfriend, Elizabeth Duncan, who was a friend of my sister Sheila. The journeys in the winter, however, were not much fun at all although the windshield provided some protection, I equipped myself with sturdy waterproofs to keep out the wind, rain and sleet, that I often had to travel through.

My mother thought I was crazy doing these journeys in foul weather as she was as terrified of my riding a motorbike as she was of my flying aircraft.

We had a training program which listed all the various performances required at each stage of one's training. This was called a RAF form which was numbered in sequence and this list had to be ticked off as each section was passed, to go onto the next one. This was all on the Percival Prentice, a twin training small aircraft.

It was very exciting when we were transferred to the bigger aircraft, The Harvard, an American manufactured aircraft which was a very good trainer. We then changed instructors to learn how to fly this aircraft. My first instructor on the Harvard was a Sergeant pilot as opposed to an officer. His name was Archie Kinch. He said, "I am a Sergeant Pilot Instructor, and you can call me "sir". So, we all knew where we stood, as it clarified the chain of discipline. He then asked my name, which I told him, and he then said he would call me "Old Boines" which he continued to do.

One of the first things Archie Kinch showed us was all around the aircraft, pointing out what to look for and the various controls that were to become so familiar to us. He demonstrated the movement of some of these controls and also the best way of and getting into the cockpit as well as how to adjust the seats and controls. He always said that the pilot must always be comfortable sitting in the cockpit.

I still vividly remember my first experiences and the procedures that were carried out.

The pupil pilot sat in the front seat, and the instructor in the seat behind the pilot with his own controls, having made sure you could reach the pedals, and that you were both strapped in securely. He would then go through the whole routine of how to go through the check list of all the procedures you had to follow before you switch the engine of the plane on. You would get the feel of the Control Stick, how it goes forward, backwards, and sideways. The forward and back movement makes the aircraft tail go up and down, the sideways movement, left and right, would make the left-hand aileron at the end of the left wing go up and down, and the righthand aileron at the end of the right wing go up and down from its neutral position. This controls the rolling of the airplane right, left or level.

The foot controls go from a neutral position to the right and left. This controls the rudder which is attached to the rear end of the tail, in a vertical position, and makes the plane turn left or right. These are the most important controls that you need to get the feel of to fly any aircraft. The configurations could vary depending on the type of aircraft.

Each foot pedal is vertical and halfway up is a horizontal hinge. The top half of the pedal hinges forward from that hinge, you apply pressure on the top half above the hinge according to how much brake pressure you want (either gently or hard). The left pedal controls the left brake, and the right pedal controls the right brake. When in the position on the runway to take off you would let your brakes off. He then explained how to start the engine by positioning the throttle, like a lever going forward or back from idle to full power. Next to that lever there was a pitch lever as well. This goes from back to forward and that adjusts the pitch angle of the individual rotating propeller blades whilst rotating with the whole propeller. Also in the cock pit is a brake lever near the joystick which is attached by what they call a Bowden cable, which pulls the brakes on the aircraft wheels, on each side of the aircraft, below the wings, on and off. This is for locking the aircraft in its position on the ground.

While the aircraft is parked each wheel has a chock in the front of the wheels of the aircraft which stops the aircraft moving on the ground. To lock the wheels, you need to pull hard on the break cabling until it clicks, as then you know it will stay on. The ropes attached are then pulled sideways by the ground crew when you are ready to move. You must see they have done so before you can taxi. Taxiing involves turning left and right, so you must use the right brake and left brake, (the lever attached to the rudder). He would then demonstrate how you would control the aircraft, by having a certain amount of power on to trickle forward, but not having too much pressure on. We would taxi left and right and forwards to get the feel of the aircraft. He would say that he would get permission from Air Traffic Control so that we can taxi on the runway to prepare for take-off. He would then say I will demonstrate a take-off for you, and you must keep your hand on your controls in order to get the feel of the take-off, while keeping your eyes on how the controls effect the movements of the plane. So, he was flying the plane, but I was able to feel as if I were.

He would then tell you that you have control, and you are to reply, "I have control". This way you always know who is controlling the plane. He has control but you can practice what he is telling you, particularly on the brakes to get the feel of them. He then said continue taxiing around turning left and right so as to recognise the feel of each movement. Then I said to him, you have control and handed the control back to him. He then responds back to me answering that he has the control. That is the basis of all discipline procedure's when you are in the aircraft.

He would then get permission from ATC (Air Traffic Control) to take off. He demonstrated how to put the power on when the brakes were off so the aircraft starts to move forward and then demonstrated how you could keep the aircraft straight as you taxied onto the runway. He then applied the power gently and the aircraft started to move forward. As he added more power the speed built up and he demonstrated again how to move the rudder left and right gently to demonstrate how effective the rudder was on the direction. As the speed built up to a higher power, he then said how he was going to ease back on the stick, and the nose of the aircraft rose just above the visual horizon, holding that altitude he put more power on and I realised we were climbing up into the air.

We then climbed to a safe height (approx. 3,000 feet above the ground) and he demonstrated to me how he could turn both left and right gently showing how the wings tilted according to your instructions. Once you reached the required attitude you put the stick control back to the neutral level and that would then hold the aircraft at that angle. He then shows again how taking the aircraft out of the neutral position, and turning to the left, turns the plane to the left to the required angle and by turning the stick control to the right, turns the aircraft to the right to the required angle. He demonstrated by doing this and when at the required angle if you returned the control stick to the neutral position it would hold the plane at that angle until you wished to change it again. Back to neutral always being the level going forward. We are then flying straight and because he is sitting in front of me and cannot see me sitting behind, he instructed me to take hold of the stick and feel how he moved the stick so that I could get the feel in the air of how it feels to turn the aircraft at the various angles.

Once I had the feel of how to control the aircraft, he would let me take control and fly the aircraft. His hand was still on "his" control to make sure I was doing the right thing. This way he could take control of the aircraft should I make a mistake.

We then climb to another level (approx. 4000 feet) and re practice putting the nose forward keeping your eye on the horizon. We undertook various manoeuvres turning left for about 10 second and then putting the aircraft level again, then turning to the right for about 10 seconds and again putting the aircraft level again. We then reduce power to pull the nose down again, hold at that attitude until the aircraft has descended back down to 3000 ft when I put the power back on and check the horizon, easing the nose back to see the horizon again through the glass windscreen of the aircraft.

We now approach the airfield; air traffic control will clear us down to 1000 ft above the ground. We carry out a circuit, at that height, at the airfield to orientate ourselves and to line up on the final approach to land. We have done our checks prior to landing making sure the flaps are in the right place, undercarriage is down, the controls all working. We descend by reducing the power to about half, and the aircraft then descends gradually while we aim at the first part of the runway. We get clearance to land from the ATC so we continue our approach and when you decide you can reach the landing point, you close the throttles, to bring the power back further. If you are going down, below the desired angle, you put a little bit of power back on to get the desired angle for lining up for the runway. At about 12 ft above the runway and you are happy with the lining up of the runway you close the throttles, bring back the power, and holding that angle as you approach the ground, ease the nose back so it goes up, and the wheels should touch down in the middle of the runway. Once on the runway, making sure you are going straight on the runway using the rudder left or right, usually gentle breaking is required. Turn off the runway and taxi to where your going to park. Put the parking brakes on and do the closing down drills of the engine. Switch off the fuel and the engines will stop. Ensure the chocks are put in place, to secure the aircraft so it does not move.

This part of my training was repeated many times until your training pilot was happy with you and your performance. Having completed this basic training, I progressed to Aerobatics.

Chapter 4 : AEROBATIC TRAINING

I was extremely excited to be starting my aerobatic training which was carried out in the more advanced Harvard training aircraft, which is a joy to fly when you get the hang of it.

The procedure involved starting with a slow roll and a barrel roll. The instructor will be sitting in the back seat and the training pilot will be in the front seat, once again the instructor has control of the controls to over-ride any error the trainee might make. He instructs you to hold the controls to get the feel of what he is doing with his control stick. He tells you the procedure you are about to do, and this is practiced until he is confident that you can move on to the next one. Once having mastered the basic easier moves, we move on to the more difficult ones like "looping the loop".

To do this procedure, you normally climb to 5 000 feet. You decrease the height, down to about 4 000 ft, you then ease back on the stick to see the horizon again. It looks like the nose is going up under the horizon, you keep pulling up and up, the horizon will be down below you by then and you continue pulling back on the stick making sure the wings are level. Continue pulling up and up and you find yourself facing straight up and you carry on going over the top of the loop. You only see the sky and you continue pulling back and when you start descending the rear side of the loop, the horizon behind you will come into view in your windscreen. You can check your correct positioning on that horizon, whether your wings are level, and you can correct that if not. Continue pulling and you will see the sky disappear and when you are over the vertical, you will see the horizon again from behind you. You focus on this one, this will rise as the nose goes down, so you are basically pointing down towards the ground. You continue pulling on the stick until the horizon is directly in front of your window. You are then level and have completed the loop and are now flying in the original direction you came from so at this stage one eases forward on the stick into the neutral position, one is then flying level and the aircraft is pointing in the original direction.

This for me was a most thrilling manoeuvre, albeit a little scary the first time of doing it.

We had to go to different airfields and one day I went to check in for my flight, and they said that Sergeant Archie Kinch was not in and had been replaced by another pilot who was a Squadron Leader. I introduced myself to him, and he said Sergeant Kinch is doing something else and I am replacing him as we often do. This is to check that other training instructors are following the correct procedures and our standards are the same. He asked if I was enjoying the course, to which I replied, "very much so, and I have a very fine instructor in Sergeant Kinch." He asked if I was any good at Aerobatics. I replied that Sergeant Kinch thought that I was pretty good. He asked me to show him some of the aerobatics that I could do. We went up in the aircraft and I had to show him the different exercises he asked for, e.g. the Loop or Barrel or Roll off the top. Once we were back, he asked if I had enjoyed the flight and he said it was nice to meet me and left. I did not realise at the time, that they were doubting Sergeant Kinch's assessments, as apparently, they were concerned that they appeared to be inflated.

Subsequently I was then sent back to the same airfield to be tested on the test course they have for low level flying. When arriving for this course, there was another pilot also doing the test. I introduced myself to him and asked which squadron he was in. He told me he was just a test pilot to check the test route was correct. He disappeared saying he would see me later and I went to the check-in office where I introduced myself to the check-in officer and he asked me to wait a few minutes for the Squadron Leader who was going to do the test of my ability to fly low levels on this course. He introduced himself to me and explained in detail the route of the course. He had a map of the course showing the route I would be taking. He said before we start, I will take you down to the starting point. He then said, I won't be coming with you as I will be standing here, because knowing the route as I do, from this position, I can see every move you do, and I can see how accurately you are flying. He then described some of the things he wanted me to do and showed me the special markers on a post and each marker is the same and you must go from one marker to the other on the route.

Low level flying would initially be at 500ft., plus or minus 100ft tolerance. The direction between 1 marker and another had to be on that line and at 500ft. The inline tolerance, being the direct line from one marker to the other, had to be in line to the tolerance of 500meters left or right of that line.

He then explained the route and how I was to pass each marker before going on to the next one because from that position he could follow my every move and assess my performance.

Once I knew what was expected of me, I took off and went to the 2nd point at 500ft. At that turning point, I turned left to the next marker, and then did a rate 1 turn to the left in a complete circle back to the starting point. I looked ahead at the next marker and turned right in a circle to face back the same way. I looked ahead to the next marker and I had to climb from 500ft to 1000ft, doing this by just easing the nose of the aircraft back a bit. At the next marker I did a right turn and started descending to 500ft again, in the turn. Then we looked ahead for another marker and that was a junction in the roads, but I ignored that because that was another junction. It was to distract me, so I carried on to the final marker, which was over a road, and proceeded to turn right and land.

I then landed and went back to the office. While I was doing this, I heard another Harvard flying and thought it was the other pilot doing his test but later heard that he was checking the route was correct. I was told where to sit and told to face him. He sat opposite me looking out at the airfield outside. I could hear that the other aircraft had landed. He then said to me "what did you think of that Mr Baines" and I replied, "very interesting, I was very nervous to begin with but settled down and enjoyed it". He replied "good" and I asked, "Have I passed sir?" and he answered "Yes you have both passed". I then saw the other pilot who I thought was being tested walking towards us, so I thought I had better get up and congratulate him. He also asked if I had enjoyed it and I said yes, he said that's good and then he said goodbye and left. It was then that I realised that he was part of the test team.

I then sat down once again with my examiner to be debriefed and he said "Now Mr Baines I have been doing this testing for over 10 years and I have passed or failed different grades". He then showed me the cards, that he had in front of him, they were all large white ones. They were all numbered in large letters, but each card was a different colour, numbered 100, 90, 75 and 60. He said on an average test I would award a pilot a number, normally either 90, 75 or 60. He then picked up the card numbered 100 and said "for your information Mr Baines I have never given this card to anyone before, it is usually the other numbers. You are the first person I have awarded it to in the whole of my career". I was shocked but very pleased when he told me well done and congratulations. He said "You never made the slightest error, and it was the most perfect check I have ever seen". I realised my mouth had dropped open so I closed my mouth and thanked him. He told me he would be sending his report into my commanding officer and thanked me again and left. I then returned back to my station. (I subsequently heard that all the other pilots in the squadron had all been watching my performance out on a nearby field).

Back at the station, I completed my flying training course up to wing standard, where I was awarded my wings, of which I was very proud.

In the meantime, Sergeant Kinch said "Old Boines I have put you in for an aerobatic competition". I was one of six pilots entered for the competition, chosen by various instructors. He told me that he would give me the sequence of events in the aerobatic competition. I could then go through the list of what they required us to do, for example, barrel rolls, slow roll and barrel roll and "flying" in one direction followed by a loop and a roll off the top, to be followed by the secret surprise operation. He then included Inverted Flying (upside down flying). However, instead of going from A to B, he wanted me while upside down to slowly turn to the left with the rudder and hold that direction, then still upside down change direction and hold that direction. Quite a challenge. His instructions to me were kept secret so no-one knew of the plan. After that I practiced the routine under his supervision. The surprise operation was going to be a N-8 - eight point roll, for example flying straight and then you roll to the left for 45 degrees (icon) and then left in a jerk action to 90 degrees then continue to 125 degrees to be followed by another 45 degrees - taking you up to a total of 180 degrees to be followed immediately with another jerk left up to 225, immediately followed left another 45 to 270 degrees to be followed to another jerk left to 315 degrees, then another 45 degrees to 360 degrees which brings you back to level after completing a full circle. The emphasis on each turn being a jerked stop and not rolling smoothly into each roll. Archie Kinch said it is important to get the 8 jerked turns. I then entered the competition as one of the 6 competitors and won it.

After completing my training, we had a special wings day. It was a big parade with family and friends attending. Names were called out individually and each pilot had to go up and have the wings badge pressed onto their left arm. He was saluted and returned to their seat. The next name was called and so it went on. However, at the end of that they mentioned the Aerobatic Trophy Competition and I was called up to receive my trophy. The Admiral made a comment that it was nice to see me again because I had already been up to receive my wings. He handed me the trophy and I saluted him and I said thank you Admiral. He then closed the ceremony, and everyone moved on to the first-class lunch and drinks.

After that you were then invited to walk across the runway where the aircraft were taking off and landing continuously so that everyone could see how it operated. My parents were very impressed, and I told them to look over to the right because this is a Harvard coming into land. We all watched it and the pilot flared the aircraft to land on its wheels, unfortunately he had his handbrake locked on, so the wheels did not rotate, and the tail of the aircraft lifted up and it went right over the aircraft turning the aircraft upside down. With the threat of a fire with all the fuel leaking out, the emergency services were there right away in case there was a fire. They broke open the aircraft and pulled the pilot out. He was still alive but badly injured. He was taken away in an ambulance. My mother then said, "good Heavens, do they often do this", to which I replied "no, thank goodness, this was a pilot error". We all returned to our table and then at the end we all went home. Regarding the pilot who made the error, he was dismissed.

My parents and my sister then drove back to the hotel where they had booked in for the night and we saw them in the morning at the hotel before they drove up to their home in Willaston, on the Wirral in Cheshire.

Chapter 5 : PROUDLY WEARING MY WINGS

On achieving my wings, I was posted down to Somerset and travelled there on my motorbike. I arrived at Royal Naval Station (RNS) and airfield at Yeovilton, ten miles from Yeovil town. I checked in with others who had arrived, and we were given our cabins and attended briefing talks about the course we were about to start on. This was under the command of Lieutenant Commander Bevan the senior instructor. We were shown around the base and settled ourselves in. The first day's lectures were on the Sea Fire 17 aircraft (identical to the RAF Spitfire 22) but with a tail wheel hook for deck landing. We looked over the aircraft both inside and out to learn all about it. We were then told before we went solo on the Sea Fire 17, we would be flown by an instructor in a Firefly aircraft. A similar looking aircraft to the Sea Fire, which we were also shown over. We had to pick up all the paperwork and pilots notes, necessary for the aircraft.

The following day, we commenced training on the Firefly and my instructor was a Lieutenant Bawden. I had him for 3 sessions on the following three days, he taught me familiarisation 1, 2 and 3. When he was satisfied with my ability to handle this aircraft, which was considerably underpowered compared to the Sea Fire, I then did my first solo, which was quite an exciting experience, because on take-off you only put about ¾ power on until you got your flying speed of about 70 knots, then rotated and nose up, increasing to normal take off power as it climbed nicely away. With the rudder fully right on the take-off which decreases as the speed built up. At a safe height I took my left hand off the throttle to take hold of the stick which I took my right hand off to reach over to the right to select the undercarriage lever up. Raising the undercarriage wheels under the wings. I then replaced my right hand back on the stick which is the normal flying position. He showed me all around the area where we would be flying up to Bath, around the south coast and the Chesil beach on the south coast. The line of the beach is perfect to learn aerobatics, like loops and barrel rolls to keep in a straight line and the countryside I got to learn for navigation purposes all around Somerset and neighbouring counties. The power of the engine was most impressive, over 2000 horsepower, a Rolls Royce Merlin Engine. It handled beautifully as you would expect a very fast fighter aircraft to do. Great fun!

Now it was my turn to fly solo, having experienced the swing on take-off from the torque of the engine and propeller combined. Over the next 3 months we had to practice various aerobatic and navigational exercises with another trainee pilot, Bungy Williams, in another aircraft flying adjacently to me. Comparing notes on how each other flew. I did notice that when I had to fly the aircraft he had flown I had to be careful to do all the checks thoroughly as he was known to push the aircrafts beyond their limits and boast about it. We always practiced in pairs, not just to compare notes but safety reasons. We also learnt close formation flying. That was also very exciting, and I enjoyed that too. We would then return to the airbase, Yeovilton, join the circuit and make a landing. This was to learn and practice "formation flying".

We then also learned "Aerobatic flying" individually. I climb to heights for example of 30,000 ft in 10 minutes to learn and feel how powerful the aircraft was. One moulded very quickly into such a fine fighter aircraft. Aerobatic flying was also learning loops and barrel rolls at a higher altitude.

We also had to practice forced landings, where you took the power off and gliding down to pick a field for landing. You would glide towards the field as if to land but put the power on again and overshoot before landing and climb away again for another exercise.

We would then practice basically the same procedure but landing on the runway and taking off again, and when you got the feel of that you would then learn a flapless landing. This where you would come into land at a much higher speed and use the brakes to slow you down. This is to give you the feel of the aircraft in different positions.

It was interesting to notice that some pilots lost control and swung off the runway as they did not have the feel of the power of the aircraft. Luckily this never happened to me.

Practicing navigation exercises would be covered. This would be approaching another airfield but not landing and just overshoot and go back. We would do this several times at different airfields. All these landings were closely watched by instructors in the towers making sure that all was done correctly. When they were satisfied with me, I was then debriefed and told I had passed satisfactory, my assessments were average, 5 out of 10 which I was very disappointed in, perhaps because I had such excellent reports and feedback on the previous training. However maybe they felt I was too confident and perhaps this was a good thing as it put me in my place. I do feel however that Lieutenant Commander Bevan relied on the other pilots notes and did my assessment relying on these, perhaps to bring me down to size: it did make me think.

Chapter 6 : OPERTIONAL FLYING SCHOOL NO 2
Royal Naval Airfield Station, Near Warrington, at Stretton, Cheshire.

The registration and documentation were similar to the previous training. We were introduced to the new Commander who was overseeing our training. His name was Lieutenant Commander White.

He had a very nice attitude and spoke to us nicely. He then explained what I was about to do at Stretton, which was an Operational flying school base, in addition to that it was also used for weekend fliers. These were naval reservists who flew there mostly at weekends. There were 2 squadrons of them, 1 fighter pilots and the other Observers/ Navigators and radio operators. He commented that as far as he was concerned, they could do with a bit of refresher training and we must not take too much notice of what they were doing.

We had our own bunks in our own cabins (bedrooms with bunks), a mess bar, toilets, refreshments, and a large dining hall for big events. Just like any other air station. We were shown around various hangers, where the aircraft were parked, runways etc. to get a feel of the base.

Lieutenant Commander White showed us the Sea Fury aircraft which we were going to fly, nicknamed the "big beastie". It was a powerful aircraft with a Bristol Centaurus engine of 2,500 horsepower (radial engine). He then proceeded to explain it in detail. He took me up in a Sea Fury Trainer 2-seater, which was very exciting and showed me the local area, which I knew fairly well anyway as it was not far from my home. He showed me forbidden flying areas and various towns and points of interest, different villages, the River Mersey and the River Dee, and the Welsh mountains about 40 miles away in the distance. He then demonstrated to me the flying of the aircraft and told me to follow him through on the controls. I found this extremely interesting and great fun. This felt like you were flying a Rolls Royce as compared to a cheaper sports car like an M G. The aircraft handled beautifully and he demonstrated various manoeuvres, letting me practice them as well. We then returned to the airfield, to join the circuits, and approach and land on the runway.

After we landed, we then went back to the start of the runway and he told me I now had control of the aircraft and told me I must show him now how to take off adding the power very gently, as it was such a powerful aircraft. I proceed to take off beautifully into the air. He selected the undercarriage up, so now the aircraft was now clean, (meaning the undercarriage and flaps if used were all tucked in the wings). I then flew around getting the feel of flying the aircraft as opposed to sitting and observing Lieutenant Commander White. We then returned to the airfield and he told me to show him how to circle and land on the runway, which I proceeded to do getting the feel of the braking system on the runway, for a successful landing. We then practised these procedures until I felt confident, then parked the aircraft, going back to the office to discuss, where he told me that I had handled the aircraft very well, which pleased me.

The next day he showed me how to navigate the aircraft using visual bearings and time legs. This is flying in a direction for say 5 minutes and then they would say look ahead and see the island in the water ahead, then instruct you to fly over it, turn left for example 180 degrees and fly in a different direction. This would be the base of the whole lesson. Then he would ask if I could find my way back, which was a challenge as I had to work out which direction to fly back to and then land. We would then return to the office and assess my lesson for the day. He then put a map on the table, to show me what we would be covering the next day. He showed me where we were, and he would draw a line on the map to whatever point he had chosen to fly to. When we got to that point, he would then show me obvious features of the next place he wanted me to fly to and then a few more. Each of these lines would be on a particular heading. You had to know what you were doing as you had to check these against your compass. On subsequent days we do similar but longer sectors to fly.

The next day I would go up with him again, with the map on my knee, folded with the section showing the route to follow was easy for me to see, I had to carry out the flight according to the map. During the flying of the route he would ask random questions like "how much fuel is left, how long can I fly on the fuel that is left?", making me learn that these things also had to be considered, not only concentrating on the directions but learning to automatically check my gauges, so that it became a habit. We landed and then once again sat and assessed my lesson for the day and then discuss the next day's lessons.

The next day we would follow the same procedure but on a much longer route and this would continue for the next few days. Every day he would challenge me with constant questions, to make me think quickly and react, without hesitation.

Once he was confident that I was able to fly solo, he then left me on my own to practice all the navigation exercises I had learnt, basically checking that I knew what I was doing and where I was going.

The next stage of this training was now to practice in the Sea Fury airplane doing aerobatics. I was left totally on my own to decide where and what I was going to practice but implementing my previous training of where I was allowed to fly and also navigating my way back, but I also had to consider the weekend pilots who popped up everywhere.

Even with taking all this into consideration, I had never had such freedom before, and I loved it.

Having completed the training, with an assessment of 7, which is above average. I then needed to stay on the reserve, for 2 years, completing my National Service at Stretton Airfield RNS (Royal Naval Station).

I was still flying in the navy at weekends until 4 November 1956 when I officially finished in the Navy.

I was told that my final Naval Assessment was stated as "Exceptional" and that only 2 Fleet Air Arm pilots, including myself, had been previously recorded at this level. It was the highest achievement that one could be granted.

Chapter 7 : FROM NAVY TO COMMERCIAL

I joined BEA on 28 November 1955 aged 20 and started my first training with BEA on 9 January 1956. When I started with BEA, I was first assigned to London for training which was basically training on the differences between flying for Nationalised Airlines as opposed to Military flying. The aircraft's now being totally different to the Naval Aircraft.

The first aircraft I was trained on was officially called a "Charlie 47" which is the same as a Douglas DC 3 or more commonly known as the "Dakota". To confuse one even more BEA chose to call it a "Pionair". Having done a ground school course in class learning all the information on the Dakota and how it worked, we would be taken out to see a parked aircraft, walk around the outside and then enter the inside of the aircraft. This aircraft contained 32 passenger seats, and they had a large fleet of these aircrafts, they were flown by 2 pilots sometimes with a radio officer. These were used mostly on short-haul flights up to 10,000 miles between England and European countries.

We flew in a Dakota, as a passenger, to Jersey an Island next to Guernsey. to the base for the flying training where they had several Dakota's available for our training. One aircraft would be used for training purposes only and the Training Captain would show us around it, explaining how everything worked. They had booked us into a Hotel for up to five nights, midweek as it was quieter, and so we were also able to relax in our free time. We were a group of approximately 10 pilots and the shifts were that 5 would work at the airport in the morning and 5 at the airport in the afternoon. We found the Training Captains also worked the same or similar shifts. What was nice and different from the military training was that in the evenings or during the day when you were off, we were able to make use of the hotels facilities and also explore the area. Having had all the military aircraft training, I had the advantage of the basic knowledge and just needed to learn how to adapt it to the way airlines operated.This training was basically the Training Captain showing you around the aircraft, going through the different flight manuals and check lists, we were also shown how all the controls worked on the Dakota. We would be shown how to start the engines and acknowledge the ground crews hand signals. The Training Captain would then call up air traffic control to get permission for a "training" take off as opposed to a "passenger take off". Once received we would taxi to the holding point before you actually go onto the runway. We would read through the check lists once again before positioning ourselves on the runway. The Captain would also open the throttle up to a certain setting to check everything was working properly, turning off each magneto switch in turn in order to see if revolutions numbers dropped as both should be more or less the same. He would ask questions to see if we understood why we were doing these checks and the reasons for them. Then we are asked if we were ready for take-off and if we were in the right position with seat belts on and if you were comfortable with the seat in the right position for comfortable access to all the controls.

He would then call for clearance for take-off, then taxi the aircraft onto the runway, and then open the throttles to take off power. The aircraft would then speed up with him having both hands on the control column holding it forward to keep it level. As the speed builds up you can see him getting the feel of the controls as the speed increases until it reaches the V2 speed (this is the speed needed to lift the aircraft off the ground). The aircraft slowly climbs nose up into the air. During the assent once you are clear of the ground, he would then instruct you to select undercarriage up, in order to tuck the wheels back under the wings and thereby also cutting the drag from the undercarriage. You would look out to check the horizon to make sure the altitude is correct and a look out in general to make sure there are no conflicting aircraft. You continue flying ahead until you reach the required altitude and then you throttle back a bit to cruising power turning right or left if needed, continuing until it is time to land. Landing is basically the same as I was taught in the Military. We would do similar things over the next 3 days with different examples of things like cross wind landings and other unforeseen obstacles one might get confronted with. We also did engine failure. The Captain would throttle back on one of the engines, causing the aircraft to swing left or right, (depending on the engine he chose). We had to keep the aircraft straight by using the Rudder and Aileron.

We then went back to London to do Line Training, (this now included passengers). This was with a Training Captain who was training me to be a co-pilot and how to follow procedures the airline way; we were flying to different countries and all around the United Kingdom. In London I was staying in digs for a weekly fee. Every day I had to go to LAP (London Airport) in my car for further training and I had a special sticker for my windscreen enabling me to park my car in the staff carpark right in the middle of the airport. There was a staff canteen in the airport for us to have a meal at any time during the day. It was a nice place to meet other pilots who were in transit to other destinations. Some were there on what was called Standby, so if needed they could call you and you were ready, standby usually being for a 5-hour period, morning or afternoon. At this time I had to fly with my Training Captain as I hadn't been cleared to fly with anyone else, as I was not classified as being fully trained. For example when I was going on a flight from London to Manchester we would check in with the FSDO (Flying Staff Duty Officer). He would give you details of your flight and crew, and other information that is relevant to the flight, He would also advise you of alterations to the flying plan if they were running late, and identification of the aircraft.

If other crew had already checked in for the flight with us. They would have had to go to a row of drawers for a flight plan for that route or a blank one. They would select their flight plans which were pre-printed or blank and go to one of the flight planning tables, spread the sheets on the table and fill in the details, names of the crew and then they would wait for the captain to come back with the met information which had to go on the flight plan. For example, the wind speed and weather information. The pilot would then indicate on the flight plan, the distance to the destination, for example 80 miles and the wind speed, and that would tell him how long the flight would take.

In addition, he would ask the captain which Alternate he would like to use for the flight planning, to calculate how much time it would take and how much fuel it would take. In addition to this, according to the flight route you would be required to take, he would ask the captain which Alternate (alternative) airport, he would like to use. He might say Birmingham, for an example, as an alternate to Manchester. The first officer had to work out how many miles that was and how long it would take to fly there and then how much fuel it would take to fly there. He would total up the time and the fuel amount and he would add to this figure 45 minutes holding fuel. Holding fuel being the amount of fuel you would need should you have to circle the airport for 45 minutes in the event of various delays. In addition to this the captain would, from his knowledge, say for example that fuel is cheaper at London than it is at Manchester and he would probably add another 200 gallons of fuel as it was cheaper. This information he would also get from the flight plan, which would indicate what the relative cost was.

Having completed all this information, we would either have a cuppa in the canteen before we left or if time was short we would go directly to the aircraft. Once at the aircraft we would get into the cockpit and meet the cabin staff if they were already there. I would have to go into the cock pit and start the pilot check list as I was the co-pilot. This was checking all the instruments etc. according to the list. The captain would go out again and check that all was in order around the aircraft, also checking that the passenger luggage was being loaded into the hold and refuelling had been completed. He would come back into the cock pit and see whether the tech log was there, check all the details had been entered correctly and also check if there were any previous snags that he needed to be aware of in order to check that they had been corrected. He would ask me if I had completed my checks and I responded "All correct sir". He would say "Ok let's get strapped in to prepare for engine start and wait for the ships papers", these are all the papers for each flight, received from the check-in staff, giving details of all the passengers, their baggage. We would check through the papers considering the total weight for take-off taking into account the estimated weight of all the passengers and the loaded luggage to check that the fuel calculations were correct. When I had checked these figures I would tell the first officer, who had his flight plan on his knee, and he would write these details down on the that flight plan.

From the figures I had given the first officer, he would check the take-off weight was within the allowed take-off weight for that flight, and that would indicate to him the V2 (which is the speed you would need on take-off) also known as the decision speed. V1 speed would be based according to which runway needed to take off, according to its length. The first officer would write this on a small firm card which is placed on top of the control panel so all the pilots could see it. We confirm with the cabin staff that all their checks are in order, once again confirm the number of passengers and that all the passengers are strapped in, and that the cabin are all set for take-off. We would check the indicator lights in the cockpit that all the doors were locked and the holding doors underneath the aircraft, where the baggage and freight is held underneath were locked. On a small airfield the ground engineer would indicate with hand signals whether it was clear to start the engine's, on a bigger airfield they would have a phone connection.

We would need to get clearance from air traffic control that we could start the engines, as there might be delays for the take off and we wouldn't sit with the engines running while waiting. Once given the all clear we would then commence the procedure of starting the engines. Once started we then get clearance to taxi and told which runway we were allocated for take-off. Once on the runway and you have your clearance for take-off, then the handling pilot who is to fly the aircraft, either the captain or the co-pilot, hold the flying controls (wheel and rudders). He then tells the non-handling pilot, to open the throttles to take off power. As the speed builds up the handling pilot would keep the aircraft going straight down the runway, taking note of the instruments that would show that the temperatures and pressures were all working properly.

When the speed reaches V1 (the decision speed) he would shout out V1. The handling pilot would then keep the aircraft on the ground, in the middle of the runway, accelerating up to V2. At V2 the non-handling pilot would say V2 and the handling pilot would pull back on the control column and rotate the aircraft to a climbing attitude (which means the orientation of the aircraft with respect to the horizon, basically meaning nose above the horizon). The aircraft would rotate to that attitude and climb up. When cleared for everything the handling pilot would call for undercarriage up. The non-handling pilot would select the undercarriage lever up and you would be able to hear the sound of them locking. You would continue climbing up to the height you cleared to and level out at the assigned altitude level. You would bring the throttles back as the speed builds up until you reach your cruising speed. Landing is the same for any aircraft.

On 24 December 1957 Captain George Roberts & I, now aged 22, flew from Renfrew (Glasgow) to Manchester. I flew that service, and he signed my logbook, as first officers very rarely handled that flight at night. As I had never flown with him before I felt it was a compliment of his faith in me.

On 21 March 1958 I was now finished flying the Dakota's and then moved on to flying a Viscount 701. The training on this aircraft I did at London Airport (renamed Heathrow in 1966). The first flight I did was London to Palma, Spain with training Captain Priest. The same day we returned from Palma to London. That flight took 3.30

hours during the day and 3.40 minutes at night. That was my first route experience with passengers. My next one I flew from London to Blackbushe without passengers, for circuit training. The same day I did a training flight with Captain Pengelli, we did circuits and full landings.

Chapter 8 : DONALDS COMMAND COURSE

Now I am fully trained and ready to fly on the line. I requested to be stationed at Manchester as it was nearer to home. I settled down there very quickly and flew with many different pilots and captains. I was treated very cautiously by them as I was a newly trained pilot by BEA. Once they got used to me, they asked me to fly the aircraft to see how I coped. This is called Route Flying. They quickly realised that I was competent because of my previous flying experience and then started giving me more to handle. I settled in and as Manchester was a small base you got to know everybody, and I had a very happy workload.

I flew with a very nice Captain called Alf French. He was like a father figure to me. He helped me with a lot of good advice and let me handle the aircraft more than any of the other Captains. Following a night stop at Belfast, we stayed at the Royal Avenue hotel, having gone in with a crew car, we would sit having a social drink in the bar, getting to know each other on a personal level. I asked him how he got into BEA and he said he was a Railway Ganga. This was a team of 6 people that would lift heavy railway lines between them, before they had machinery to do this. He was called up for his Military Service and was given a choice of the Army or the air force and he chose the air force and he was trained to be a pilot flying an Oxford Twin Engine Communication Aircraft. After completing his Military Service, he went back to being a Railway Ganga as they had to hold his job open after the war. While he was walking along the railway line one day, with another Ganga, this light twin aircraft flew across fairly low, in front of them. He mentioned he used to fly those in the RAF. The friend suggested he should apply to BEA, which was down the road and advertising for Pilots. He applied and that is how he became a BEA pilot.

In the days when I was flying on some of the short haul routes we had flight clerks, (not stewardess). The difference between a flight clerk and a stewardess is that there was no catering at all on these flights. They however had to do the same security checks before take-off and landing, making sure that the passengers were all settled and strapped in and the doors were closed etc.

I was here for approximately 1 year and as they were replacing the Dakotas with the Vickers Viscount 701, I had to go to London for a short course to learn about the differences between flying the Dakota and flying the Vickers Viscount 701. This took about 3 weeks of training, with different training captains, and a radio officer, as part of the crew, which was always needed on a long-haul flight. This training was base training of circuits and landings with no passengers and then line training with passengers, The Vickers Viscount 701 held 47-53 passengers so was slightly bigger than the Dakota, which only held up to 32. It also had 4 engines as opposed to 2 on the Dakota. Once I had completed this training and still based in London with the Line Training Captains, we flew from London to many different places. Nice, Rome, Malta, Athens, Cyprus then often from there across to Beirut in Lebanon, the next day we would fly across the Saudi Arabian dessert to Kuwait. The temperature here was uncomfortable and very hot, about 140 degrees centigrade. After several days there we would return on a similar route to London, often taking a week each way. Having done a few of these routes, I had completed my training on this Aircraft and returned to Manchester to fly the Vickers Viscount 701 there.

In March 1959 they then changed the Vickers Viscount 701 to the Vickers Viscount 800 series, slightly bigger holding 69. I had to follow the same procedure by going to London for the training on this aircraft and continued as a first officer at Manchester where I was very settled.

It was on the 24th of May 1960 that I married my wife Barbara at St. Winifred's Church in Neston where Barbara came from. We had a wonderful reception at the Leighton Court Country Club before flying off to Spain on our honeymoon, spending one night in

Barcelona followed by an idyllic week at a beautiful hotel called Xalok (pronounced Chalock) on the beach front at Playa d'Aro.

I recall the first time I met Barbara and for me it was love at first sight. I had gone with my friend Chris to the Park Gate Cricket Club where he was meeting his girlfriend, Marjorie. When I was introduced to Marjorie I asked her "Are there any more like you at home?" to which she replied that yes there was as she had an elder sister. "Go home and fetch her" I said, which Marjorie did and that was the start of my romance with Barbara whom I courted for 5 years before marrying.

During our courtship Barbara and I had spent many an hour talking about and planning the sort of house we would love to live in and once married we decided that we would build our dream home ourselves in a place called Goostrey in Cheshire. It took four years to build, which I did in my free time, and meanwhile we lived in a large comfortable caravan on the site. We could see the Jodrell Bank Radio Telescope about 2 miles away in the distance. When completed we had a beautiful four bedroomed house with separate garage and outbuildings, we named the house Iago, after Porth Iago, a lovely beach in North Wales. We were extremely fortunate in our neighbours Raymond and Marie Gould who became good lifelong friends; I became Godfather to their daughters Annabel and Gabrielle: we are still very much in touch to this day.

It was in 1963 that I had a very bad car accident and fractured my spine and broke 6 ribs. I was on crutches for 6 months and was unable to work for that period. I kept myself busy doing the house as best I could although it was very slow progress.

I continued flying as first officer until 12 December 1966. I had been flying with many senior officers and what I had not realised was that they were assessing me, to see if I made the grade to become a Captain. I obviously made the grade as I was sent on a Command Training course to Jersey. I was flown, as a passenger, to Jersey where we were interviewed and put up in a hotel once again, while doing our command training. We would do circuits, take-offs and landings etc. at Jersey for 3 or 4 days. Once we had the basics we would take off from Jersey and fly south to Dinard, France. Other days we would go to Cherburg, France. The reason being they hand runways pointing in different directions. I would sit in the left had seat and have complete control of the plane. The Training Captain would sit in the right-hand seat to instruct me.

In 1967, 11 years after joining BEA, I received my Command and became a Captain on the Viscount 800 series.

We were very settled in Manchester, with me having built our home and now the expected birth of our baby. Everything seemed to be going so well and then BEA decided to put the BAC1-11 a twin-engine aircraft to be based at Manchester. This meant that, although I was a captain, more senior Captains, from London, wanted to bid for the positions to fly these aircrafts in Manchester. I was a very Junior Captain at that time. The other more senior Captains from London wanted to apply for these positions as flying this aircraft paid a lot more money and being Senior Captains they had higher rank to enable them to get the positions. This meant that I would have to move from Manchester to somewhere else leaving or selling our house. They then gave me notice to leave Manchester and move to London flying the Trident 3 or to Gatwick with B.A. Air Tours flying the old Boeing 707s. I told them that I was not able to move at that time mainly because my wife was pregnant however she was not having a very good pregnancy and it was not advisable for her to move. They then agreed to let us stay there for another 6 months to see what the outcome would be. After the 6 months, the property market was so bad that we could not sell the house, also the Senior Captains from London were hoping to commute to Manchester as they did not want to sell their houses in London. This meant they would have to fly daily to and from London as a passenger on a staff ticket or to drive their own car approx. 200 miles each way at their own expense.

After a difficult pregnancy Barbara and I were blessed with the birth in August 1969 of a daughter whom we named Lucinda. I described her arrival as "the icing on the cake" in that I had a beautiful wife, a fabulous home and a job which I absolutely loved, and an adorable baby girl. I was indeed a very lucky young man.

CHAPTER 9 : THE MOVE DOWN SOUTH

I remained in Manchester for a while, however I was eventually forced to leave after Barbara had given birth to our first child. This move as earlier mentioned was due to the higher-ranking pilots taking the flights that went out from Manchester, earning themselves a higher pay packet. I was very sorry to be leaving as I had made many friends in the area as well as having built our "dream" home. I have so many happy memories of living there.

However, we had to leave and so Barbara, Lucinda and I moved to the South of England, to a village called Tilford, near Farnham in Surrey.

Here we took over a house which had been rather badly built and had many faults, but it was selling at a very good price and it gave us the opportunity of remodelling it to make it our own. The house was called Westwood, sitting in a plot of roughly two acres, and as well as giving attention to the house we were able to create a most beautiful garden with a pond, or indeed one might say a small lake with fish.

I created a water system so that the flow of the water from the stream, which ran across the rear of the garden, would flow into the pond one side and out the other. We endowed the garden with many specimen trees also building a summer house where we spent many an hour barbequing. We created a large vegetable patch where we regularly harvested our crops of potatoes, onions, beans, etc, as well as having many fruit bushes.

The property backed on to Hankley Common and we had a gate in the rear fence which gave us direct access, a wonderful place for walking and letting our dog have a good run.

Our home in Tilford was the venue for many, many, parties and social family/friend gatherings, Barbara being truly a first-class hostess and an excellent cook and we both loved entertaining. We held an annual Christmas Eve party for family, friends and neighbours, it was open house and often had 80 or more people. As Lucinda got older, she proved a great help following in her mother's footsteps in being a great cook and hostess.

The location of the house was ideal for my work with Heathrow to the west being only an hour away, and with Gatwick to the east roughly the same distance. We could also be down on the South Coast in roughly the same time. We were fortunate in the neighbourhood we had chosen as it was extremely friendly. We settled in well making lots of new friends as well as having many of my airline colleagues living nearby. It was a lovely rural spot with a local shop/post office and the town of Farnham being only 5 miles to the north where one could get the train directly up to London. Another largish town nearby was Aldershot, a military town, headquarters of the British Army and just a little further north the town of Farnborough, a very famous airfield, which holds the Farnborough International Air show annually, an event I frequently attended.

We were very fortunate in having excellent neighbours either side of our property with Sir Ernest Harrison and his wife Jane one side of us and Tom and Yvonne Hammond in Winding Wood on the other. When Tom and Yvonne sold in 1983 a young couple Maureen and Alastair bought the house. They had two children, James and Matthew, and the family all became our great friends, with whom we spent many a fun time, such happy memories. James is now Godfather to my first grandchild Oscar.

We went on many holidays abroad, Barbados being a particular favourite of ours, more than often travelling in First Class, an advantage of being a Captain with the airline. We also tried to visit friends abroad like Dennis and Marion Woods, when they were living down in France, Dennis being a pilot friend since 1969 whom I had trained. We enjoyed a wonderful catamaran holiday with them and other friends Neil and Bettie sailing around the Turkish coast. Canada was a place we enjoyed very much when we visited old neighbours of ours from Tilford who had moved out there. Our visits to Cypress with Barbara's cousin George and Margaret Hughes and their children were great fun and we very much enjoyed the beautiful sunshine and the warm seas to swim in.

A favourite type of holiday was touring the wine regions with our long-standing friends Raymond and Marie Gould, our original neighbours, as we all had an interest in and a taste for good wines.

During this period, the demand for flights was low so I had a lot of spare time on my hands. I was then able to spend a lot of time doing all that needed to be repaired on the house. Barbara, Lucinda, and I would also take daily outings exploring the countryside and towns around us. We regularly headed back up North to visit my parents in the Williston area and Barbara's parents who lived in Parkgate, very close to the River Dee, Cheshire. The drives were long, however they loved to see us and of course lovely Lucinda. On occasions my father and mother would travel down to visit us.

Lucinda had a love for animals especially dogs and horses. We encouraged her regarding her love for horses by enrolling her in a local riding school which she loved and became very good at it.

Our first dog was a miniature white poodle called Bianco, he was my wedding gift to Barbara and very special to us. We were extremely sad when he died but he had a good life. We went to look at various dogs and we saw a standard white poodle which Barbara fell in love with and we named him Champers. (Short for Champagne, of course!!). Then later came Shandy, also a male white standard poodle, followed by Clicquot who was also a white standard poodle, however he grew into a huge dog and was unbelievably intelligent. (note the connection to Champagne !!!!) I spent a lot of time training Clicquot and he was exceptionally well trained and obedient. Lucinda used to ride a neighbour's friend's horse (Minstrel) in their field, I would take her there and walked with her while she gently rode around the field. I used to put a little pile of small sticks and this horse obviously had an idea of jumping over them and eventually, I could line up a few lines of them and they would jump over them, which she loved. Lucinda went to the local village school in Tilford. I used to take her to school but if I was away flying, then Jane Macintyre would pick up Lucinda and drop her off at home as she was dropping her children. Jane and her husband Ian were very good friends and the children often played together. Their children were Kate and Emma. Lucinda was very happy at the school and had a lot of friends. She was well liked by the teachers. They used to have annual Christmas concerts, plays and parties.

Lucinda was a very sociable child with lots of friends; we always had a houseful of children. She kept us extremely busy with her social life, engagements, and commitments. After leaving school she attended Eggleston Cookery College where she trained and qualified as a Cordon Bleu Chef. She excelled in this field and cooked for many shooting and fishing parties, as well as Directors' luncheons in the City, also taking a live-in position as a chef with a lovely couple Lord and Lady Euston, where she travelled between their London and country homes. She had a love of travelling and in 1991 took herself off around the world, stopping off in Singapore, Australia, New Zealand, Fiji and the U.S.A. a most wonderful trip for her.

However, I digress from my main story about my time and experiences as a pilot.

Chapter 10 : 1970 : FROM VISCOUNT TO TRIDENT

After five years of being a Captain still flying the Viscount, I was promoted to learn to fly the Trident 3, this was on the 13th of December 1972. It was on the 9th of March 1973 I flew to Preswick to do the base training course on the Trident 3. The other Captain with me, also to train was a Captain by the name of Joe Cunningham. We did the base training until the 14 March 1973. For 4 days we did various circuits, including 2 engine and 1 engine plus the boost engine on or off. On the last day we undertook droopless landings, which are high speed landings.

From completing the base training, we went onto line training with different training captains in London. Line training included many different routes mainly to and from London but some to and from Manchester. We covered many places in Europe and the middle east, also to Scandinavia.

The rest of my time on Trident 3 flying these routes and others were all now with passengers. I was then asked to be a training captain on the Trident 3 because of all my experience on the Viscount. From then on, I was training a variety of pilots, some new entry pilots, some pilots converting from other aircraft types, on to the Trident 3. Some senior first officers on Command courses on the Trident 3 and training captains on the other aircrafts on the Trident 3. This was a very interesting time as there were many amusing and interesting events and happening during some of the flights not only the commercial flights but the special charter flights that I flew. My cabin address was always my strong point as people always appreciated my honesty, explanations, and apologies, particularly on the charter flights with many different well-known passengers, who appreciated the fact that I took the time to come and talk to them personally. Plus, I flew some royals. Many passengers personally thanked me but many took the time to write to the Airline and my flight manager always gave me a copy of them to keep. I found this very flattering.

I will never forget the one time we had "the Prime Minister" on board. Ted Heath was part of this particular charter although not as the Prime Minister but as part of the LSO (London Symphony Orchestra). I introduced myself to him, he was very hard to talk to and it was very awkward, I did however notice, which I also found quite amusing, that he was drinking one of the top First-Class Malt whiskeys. I then moved on and I went back to Andre Previn (the famous conductor of the Orchestra) and I mentioned that he might know my uncle, Gerry Mac Donald. He was very surprised, and he told the rest of the orchestra, many of whom also knew him. What they didn't know was that my uncle organised many of my charter flights for many different Orchestra's over the years as I had made a requested to him that I would like to do any available chartered flights from BEA, as they were more interesting to me.

One of my Royal flights, I will always remember was flying the crown Prince Akihito of Japan and his wife Princess Michiko (a very beautiful lady) from London to Edinburgh in the morning and then to Cardiff. There was a lot of effort from British Airways for this flight. With hospitality departments that were part of British Airways that I had never heard of before, organising various things besides the standard security and media coverage etc. On this flight, I walked around the aircraft but this time I had a translator with me. I welcomed everyone and then I went to welcome the prince who introduced me to his wife and then also the other people travelling close to him. I walked around with him through the aircraft. A short period after this flight my flight manager, called me in and said he had a letter for me which was from the Prince and Princess thanking me for the flight and enclosed was a personal gift for me. It was a set of silver spitfire shaped cufflinks. According to BEA rules we were not allowed to accept gifts from passengers so I had told the flight manager Les Wallis, that I cannot accept gifts and he said I am glad you know the rules Captain, however I am giving you a direct order to accept the gift because if you did not accept them, it would be an insult to the Prince. I told the Flight Manager that I am a training captain, and I should set an example to all, but thank you for authorising the gift and I accepted it. Still to this day I wear the cufflinks whenever I need to.

Another well-known passenger was Julie Andrews. One of my wife's and my all-time favourites. I went to her and said, "how nice to see you on board" and tell her that it was an honour to meet her in person. She was even nicer in person and she thanked me for coming to see her.

Another of my favourites was David Niven the film actor who was always very friendly.

I recall a not so pleasant flight, where the steward came up to see me to tell me that they had an awful passenger who had drank to much and had been rude to the stewardess who was in tears. I then told the steward to let the passenger know that I, (the captain) would be coming shortly to see him and make sure he was strapped in his seat. Insisting that the Steward, made it clear to the passenger that he needed to calm down and make sure he was strapped in. When I went to see the passenger, I asked him what his problem was and asked him what his job was. I then told him that he is in privileged seating and he should behave as such, because there are only 20 passengers in first class and a total of 350 on the aircraft. The aircraft cabin staff must allocate time to each passenger on board, no matter which class they are travelling in. I told him I knew what his problem was (challenging him) and said that he was frightened of flying and he was shocked and asked how I knew. I told him that after many years of flying I knew the signs when I saw them. I then told him that there would be no more alcohol for him and if he didn't behave from now on, I would divert the aircraft to Paris. The reason I was doing that is because he was endangering the safety of the aircraft and passengers, and I would then be handing you over to the customs and the French police (who were known to extremely strict and stand no nonsense from anybody.) What follows would be up to them, but you won't be coming home as you will be staying there for a while. He went very quiet. So, I told him that one more and I will do just that. After my written report to management, they would decide on his future, whether they would allow him to fly on their flights. I told him the cabin staff will be watching him and if there were any more problems than I would carry out my emergency landing at Paris. I told the cabin staff that I threatened him, but I would carry it through. When we landed, he would not get off the airplane as we had our jobs to do and when we were ready then I would go see him again. He wanted to say he is sorry, and I accepted his apology, but he was not to do it ever again. I told him I would send my report to Management and it was for them to decide what action they wanted to take. Luckily these incidents were very rare.

Diversions to different airports were rare and mostly for medical reasons. If someone is taken ill on the flight, we always ask if there is a doctor on board to make himself known to the cabin staff. If they were not able to assist, we would then have to divert to the nearest airport for medical attention. Luckily in all my years of flying, only once did I actually have a passenger die. The cabin staff had to cover him up and strap him in his chair until we landed. Not very pleasant but unfortunately that is all we could do.

On a lighter note, one very amusing experience I had was with another Captain. He needed a co-pilot on a very short trip, as the co-pilot who normally flew with him, had a previous commitment so could not make it. I offered to be the co-pilot for him. We flew to Malta and on the way back, as we had no passengers on the return flight, the Captain offered to show me interesting bays and small inlets etc. surrounding Malta. He was only flying at 500 feet, which is the minimum height over water, for me to have a better view. He then asked if I had ever seen the Nudist Colony beach, which I replied no. We were flying into the sun and as we approached the beach, we could see it was empty, except for a couple who obviously thought they had total privacy to show their love for each other!!!! AS the sun and the wind were coming from the South East towards us, they could not hear the aircraft. He then aimed to fly over them and with the noise of the four engines and propellers on the Viscount, they got the fright of their lives. The captain then lifted and went over the hill ahead of us and flew back to Luqa where the International Airport was for Malta.

We used to fly, from Malta, approx. once a week, mostly a businessman trip, with 2 stewards on board and normally also freight included on the flight, from Malta to Tripoli, in Libya and back. Approx. an hour and a half one way. When we arrived at Tripoli airfield, in the desert, with very basic buildings, we would park in our allocated space. If passengers got off they had to walk quite far to the small building (more like a shack) and their luggage would be taken off and taken across to the building with a truck.

On one particular trip, when I was the Captain, when we landed, I called the Steward aside and I said to him, that he must lock the bar because when the custom officers get on, they expect to find the bar open, so then they would be able to help themselves to all the bottles of miniature spirits, as alcohol was forbidden in Libya and they could sell them. I told him it was a direct order from me, as the Captain. When they questioned why it was locked, I then told them that as Captain on this aircraft I know what is going on and that I am going to report what is going on to British Airways head office in London. He got off empty handed.

I had got into a routine with my co-pilots when BEA approached me and offered the base training captains' course, to become a Base Training Captain. A Base Training Captain was a captain who trained other Captains, First Officers, or pilots. This training was flying without passengers. This was my ultimate dream. To become a Base Training Captain and on my favourite of the aircrafts up to then flying and teaching on the Viscount 800 series.

I ended the Viscount Base Training in late 1972 and then started flying the Trident 3B, Base Training at Prestwich on 9th March 1973 until January 1977. Then after 2 months training, I went on to the Tristar my first flight being again at Prestwich on the 28th of March 1977.

Chapter 11 : Blind Landing

I really enjoyed my time as a training captain on the Trident 3 and from the log books that I still have I see that I trained 974 pilots of all different levels. The aircraft was highly technical with a triplex system of 3 different auto-pilot units that were interconnected.

From the Trident 3 I then went on to fly the Tristar L-1011 made by Lockheed.

It was on the 2 November 1978 and I was Captain on a flight due to fly into Charles De Gaulle airport, the main airport in Paris, the other being Orly about 21 miles away. I was told that visibility in France was very bad and that the whole area was covered by low cloud. The Tristar and myself had what is known as Category III clearance. This basically means that one has authority to undertake a precision instrument approach and landing with no decision height or a decision height lower than 100ft (30m) and a runway visual range not less than 700 ft(200m). I made sure the rest of the crew were also Category III and we took off heading for the De Gaulle airport.

On approaching Charles De Gaulle I radio contacted the Airport Tower to enquire about conditions for landing. The response that I was given was a Category II clearance, that being a precision instrument approach and landing with a decision height lower than 200ft (60m) but not lower than 100ft (30m), and a runway visual range less than 2400ft (800m) but not less than 1200ft (350m).

I queried this instruction pointing out that we had the Category III status but they said we know who you are but we are giving you our own limits which are Category II. I asked them whether that also applied to the Air France flights to which they made comment "No, they are not landing anyway". It was a very much take or leave it attitude which I was surprised to hear.

I told the Tower that I was going to inform the ICAO (International Civil Aviation Organisation) that they had down-graded us from Cat 111 to Cat 11 and that it was illegal but basically the response from them was that we could do what you want. I informed them that I would make a Cat 11 approach and if necessary overshoot. Flying the aircraft to the Cat II level in an attempt to land I did have to give instruction to over-shoot. I instructed the then 3rd co-pilot to check Orly Airport to see they were Cat 111 and this he did; the

response was that yes they were accepting Cat III so I made the decision that we would go there. We confirmed with Orly that we were diverting giving them our co-ordinates and they gave authority to proceed and instructions to tune in to their 'Localiser'; this is an instrument landing system of horizontal guidance which is used to help provide lateral and vertical guidance to the pilots when landing an aircraft. It works by sending 2 beams up from the landing runway, one telling the pilots if they are high or low and the other telling them if they are left or right on the runway centreline.

I then instructed the crew to get ready for landing which required all the correct checks to be made ensuring the auto pilots and all electronics were working fully. With the aircraft made ready we descended using the triplex auto pilots making the approach with the appropriate flap settings and engine power following down the glide path. We radioed Orly and asked what the runway visual range was (this is known as the RVR) and were told it was -400 metres, then -600 metres.

As the aircraft descended, we came below 2,000 ft and at 1,800 ft we broke downwards out of the cloud which was above us however below right across the airfield was a blanket of fog. We could see the control tower and other buildings standing out above the fog, also I saw the radio mast standing high and it recognised it as the transmitter mast and therefore knew I was in the correct place at Orly.

When we reached 1,000 ft I informed the crew that we would make the attempt to land and if not possible then we would overshoot. One of the co-pilots had one of the electronic auto pilot boxes in front of him and the other sitting next to him had a similar box which was the overshoot box. We were tuned into the Orly Localiser and the aircraft was making its decent in the fog. At 15 feet the co-pilot asked for the final decision, with all 3 auto pilots in agreement I gave the command to Land which committed us to making the landing even though the ground was still completely covered in fog. The airplane gave a little shudder and then the nose went slightly up which indicates that the wheels are coming down and then very shortly afterwards we could feel the wheels hit the runway and we safely landed the aircraft.

Having carried out this manoeuvre in an Aircraft Simulator many times this was my very first actual experience of what is known as a 'blind landing' and it was both thrilling and exhilarating. Having kept the passengers informed of the difficulties with the fog and landing issues, they gave a great cheer when we safely landed at Orly and on leaving the aircraft many gave their thanks to the crew. The aircraft was carrying 20 first class passengers, 267 tourists and 15 cabin crew. The French Air Traffic control gave us their congratulations and I was able to claim the record for the first zero visibility landing at Orly Airport having carried out this 'blind landing'.

On our return to London we found that the blind land news had already reached there and in our communications with the Air Traffic Control Tower in London we were given their congratulations. On landing we were surprised to hear the ground crew express their admiration and it seemed that everyone was very impressed with what we had done.

Another flight which I have been able to recall from looking at my log books and some of the wonderful letters that were sent to me is the time the aircraft I was Captaining was hit twice by lightening. It was on 1st May 1979.

I was actually at home in Tilford on Standby when I got a call asking me to make myself available for a flight from London to Athens. I was told that there had been very bad weather which had already caused a 4 hour delay. I headed straight for the airport and when I got there I obtained all the flight details and asked where the passengers were being held. I went directly there and made an address to the passengers advising them who I and my crew were and explaining to them that unfortunately there would be further delays as the aircraft that had come in to take them to Athens had to be checked over before any departure could be made. The Incoming Captain told me that he had noted in the record book the "acceptable deferred defects" of the aircraft. I asked him where he had come from and what exactly were these defects, one of which was the de-icing equipment. That is not an acceptable defect for me I told him as we were due to fly the aircraft into horrendous weather down to Athens. The ground crew were instructed to get an engineer working on the plane but I was advised it was going to take a considerable time. I then checked when the next aircraft would be available and was told this would not be for another hour. I again went and addressed the passengers and told them the situation that the plane which had arrived was not suitable which meant that most regrettably there would be a further delay until a new aircraft arrived and was made ready.

Eventually we take off and head on down to Athens where the weather was not good at all and on approach we could see thunder and lightning all above the airport. Fortunately myself and my co-pilot were well experienced in flying in very bad weather. We were carrying out the normal approach procedure when the right wing of the aircraft had a direct lightening hit, then shortly afterwards there were two more lightening hits which took out some of the radar electronics so we were working with basic equipment. I made the decision to overshoot the Athens airport as the visibility was so terrible and we couldn't see the runway: we rose up to 4,000 turning left in to a holding position.

After communicating with the Control Tower at Athens we got clearance to head on to Thessaloniki (Greece's second largest city) which was about 50 minutes flying distance away, where weather conditions were much better. I advised the passengers what was happening and we went on to land successfully without any problems at Thessaloniki.

I say without any problems, but we soon found that there was in fact quite a big one in that the airport did not have any passenger landing steps that would fit the aircraft which was a Tristar! Their suggestion was that they refuel the aircraft and we then fly it back to Athens however I and my crew were not able to do this because we had flown the maximum hours allowed and wouldn't be able to fly again until 2.00 pm the next day. After much verbal deliberation the problem was eventually sorted by the ground crew borrowing steps from the Military Airbase next door to the airport, which made it possible for the passengers to exit the plane.

Just before we had started the flight in London, almost at the last minute, we had a visit into the cockpit from an Airport Official carrying a small briefcase who told me that this was valuable cargo which should have gone into the secure location in hold number 1 but that everything was closed up. In order to save further delay having the hold opened I said that as it was small enough I would carry the cargo under my seat in cockpit where it would be safe enough. The valuable cargo was in fact gold bars. Thessaloniki Airport may not have had any steps ready for our aircraft on arrival but they did have someone standing by to immediately relieve us of the valuable cargo!

Chapter 12 : My Flying Days Finish

It was in 1979 that I started suffering from terrible headaches and although I kept going back to the BA doctors they could not find the problem. Eventually I went to a private specialist who was recommended as being at the top in his field. There were only 2 places in England who did the CT scans at that time, the Middlesex Hospital in London and the other one was a private one on the North Circular Road. I was sent there to have the CT scan and certain tests, the doctor advising me to take my cheque book with me.

They found that I had a blockage in my brain and that I needed an operation which I had in 1980 (this operation had never been done on someone of my age before, only children) putting in a ventricular shunt. My condition was discussed with a group of other neurosurgeons and they explained the risks involved. I decided to take my chances and have the procedure. The ventricular shunt was inserted and the next day I was fine. However sadly because of this I lost my civil flying licence. It was thought that the bad car accident I had back in 1963 had been the cause of the hydrocephalus.

As was common practice with many pilots I had taken out a private insurance policy to cover me for loss of my flying licence, it included many different reasons. However, when it came down to my claiming for the £30,000 cover, they said they would only pay £18,000 as they classed my situation as a mental problem, not recognising the true medical issue involved. This was not acceptable to me and I challenged the insurance company.

If I wasn't going to be able to fly then I wanted to still be involved with flying and applied for a position with the Air Accident Investigation Unit at Farnborough, the famous airfield. I went to a friend and neighbour Sir Peter Fletcher and we discussed what had happened with the loss of my flying licence and also the insurance issue. Peter mentioned that he was on the Board and would put in a good word for me. Unfortunately, I was turned down for the position. They refused me on the grounds that the two previous occupants of that position, (inspectors of the accidents) had both omitted to mention that they had certain medical problems and therefore all future candidates must have a clear medical history. Peter came back and told me that they could not accept my medical history which showed the ventricular shunt brain problem and all the plastic plumbing down the body for the drainage of the shunt. This decision was sent in writing to the insurance company who then agreed that it was the true reason for my license loss and they agreed to pay me the full claim of £30,000. This was in 1981.

I had been a member of Hargreaves Lansdowne, Financial Advisors for a few years already so I spoke with Steven Lansdowne, who I had spoken to before, and told him that I would like his advice on how to invest this money. He offered to come and see me to discuss my financial requirements. He explained that there was no fee for his advice and suggestions however when I had decided on what I wanted to do with the advice given, a fee would be charged at the normal stock market fee.

I then invested the insurance money received although slightly less than the full amount. Since then the value of those shares has gone up and has given me a very good consistent return on my investment and this is why I recommend them.

No longer being able to fly I decided to put my house building skills to work and started up a Company which was titled Baines Property Services, handling all manner of building related issues and general maintenance. I project managed various large house extensions, as well as helping various elderly people with routine maintenance of their properties. I was kept very busy and enjoyed this period of my life, albeit I very much missed the flying. I eventually decided to fully retire in 1996.

Over the years, the shunts had to be replaced. The first one lasted about 2 years and then the terrible headaches came back so they again had to replace the shunts, the 6th one being approximately 1996. It was however in 1999 that I had a stroke, this was due to one of the earlier shunts causing a clot. I was very lucky as it was caught quickly and treated. I had another stroke in 2016 which unfortunately left me with a weakness on my left side, I was given a series of exercises which I need to regularly undertake.

I recall many a happy day at Westwood for instance Lucinda's 21st party held in the garden in 1990, but perhaps the most memorable being the wedding of our daughter Lucinda to Guy Pause on the 18th July 2003. Lucinda had met a South African man and they flew to and from South Africa while they were dating. In February 2003 while she was visiting Guy in South Africa, he proposed to Lucinda and in March 2003 he flew over to the UK to ask for Lucinda's hand in marriage.

It was a most wonderful occasion; we held the reception for over 100 guests in a beautiful marquee in our garden where the sun shone and even Concorde flew over whilst people were having drinks on the lawn. Many of the guests believed me when I jokingly said that I had organised it especially. Both Barbara and I being extremely fond of our son-in-law Guy, eventually forgave him for taking our daughter abroad to South Africa to live.

Two years after Lucinda's wedding, in April 2005 we moved to Emsworth to be by the sea. We moved in and then took ourselves immediately off to South Africa as Lucinda had given birth to Oscar my first grandson, on 8 April 2005, my second grandson Benjamin being born 4 years later on the 9 March 2009. It greatly pleases me that both grandsons are not only really good academically but also good at a variety of sports and they have a passion for boating and skiing. Standing above all these achievements however is the fact that they are both kind, considerate, helpful young people.

The 4 bedroomed home we bought in Emsworth also required certain modifications and on our return from our visit to South Africa we set about making the adjustments we wanted to make the property "ours". As with our previous home we also created an interesting garden with specimen plants and a few trees. It is a lovely part of the country and Barbara and I were very happy with the move.

We continued with our holidays abroad and visited South Africa many times to enjoy time with our daughter and the family. We were lucky that they also enjoy coming over to England which they do every year.

Although life was really very good for Barbara and I unfortunately ill health, mainly due to our getting older, started to curtail our freedom. Barbara was diagnosed with Type 2 Diabetes which was controlled with medication and diet changes. Later, she was diagnosed with Breast Cancer and she declined an operation taking a medicinal course of treatment instead. Sadly, even though she was a very strong person and a fighter, we eventually had to employ a full-time career to assist her. Sadly, toward the end of March 2020 she was admitted to Hospital with a brain haemorrhage and a stroke. With all the Covid restrictions at that time, I was not able to be with her and she passed away in the hospital without regaining consciousness on the 4th April. Barbara would have been 90 on the 28th May 2020 and it would have been our 60th wedding anniversary on the 24th May 2020.

Barbara's funeral was a very small affair, only 6 in attendance due to the Covid restrictions, however it was available on a computer live link which enabled my daughter Lucinda and her family in South Africa to watch the ceremony as it happened. For the funeral I wore my airline captain's uniform, including cap, as Barbara had always said she loved to see me in my uniform which she had always meticulously laid ready for me in my flying days.

I consider myself to have been a very lucky man indeed to have had the love and care of such a wonderful woman for so many years and I am sure you can imagine what a loss it is to me that she is no longer here.

I also have had numerous health issues, the most devasting however was the news that I had the onset of Alzheimers. My mind gets befuddled at times especially with short term memory, names, etc. and it is very frustrating when one cannot give a clear voice to the words one wants to say.

I am fortunate that I am still able to live in my own home with the assistance of a fulltime career and with the loving support of my daughter and her husband who handle the more administrative matters that life involves.

As mentioned in my note at the beginning of this "My Story" I have found that with concentration on my past life the memories have come flooding forward. A visit (pre Covid) to the Air Sciences Museum at Farnborough Airport, with my old pilot friend Dennis Woods, was an absolute joy especially as we were fortunate enough to be invited into the cockpit of their refurbished Trident three (G-AWZ1) which I had personally flown. From my own log-books I was able to provide them with information on various flights that I had taken in the aircraft which they then entered into the museum Aircraft Log Book. It is a fascinating museum well worth a visit; so many happy memories came back to me.

This story (which I have written with the help of various people) will be an aid for my memory in future years. Should any profit be made from sales of this book they will be donated to charity.

Thank you for reading "Donald's Story".

The End.

AIRCRAFTS FLOWN BY DONALD

Whilst serving in the Navy :

Percival Prentice
North American Harvard
Fairy Firefly Mark 1
Seafire Mk17 *(Navy equivalent of the Spitfire, adapted for operation from aircraft carriers)*
Hawker Seafury
Sea Vampire T22
Supermarine Attacker FB2
Airspeed Oxford Mark 1
Sea Balliol T21
Sea Prince
Dominee (Rapide)
De Havilland Sea Venom FAW

Whilst serving with the Commercial Airlines B.E.A. and B.A. British European Airways existed until 1974 when it merged with BOAC to become British Airways.

Dekota Charlie 47 (DC3)
Vickers Viscount 701
Vickers Viscount 702/6
Hawker Siddeley Trident 3
Lockheed Tristar L-1011

As a passenger I have flown in many different aircrafts, but the two most memorable were when 2 separate friends took me up into the air in their de Havilland Tiger Moth and an Auster Autocrat

PICTURES WHICH MAY BE OF INTEREST

The advertisement in the Liverpool Daily Post, 10th October 1953 which started my career.

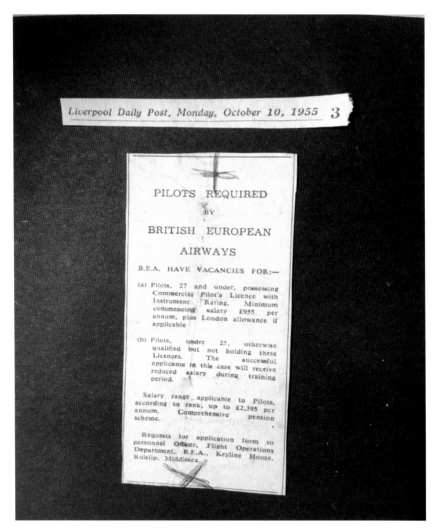

I thoroughly enjoyed my time at school, and particularly loved the sport. I was very proud when I was chosen to play for the 1st 15 Rugby Team at St. Mary's College. The photograph below, taken in 1950, shows me at the end of seated row on the right.

The picture below was taken at Gosport where I did my pre-flight training. It shows me in the Seafire 17.

I had such great fun flying with the Aerobatic Display Crew at Stretton. On one occasion the Duke of Edinburgh came to an event to see the display. That's me standing on the right of the photograph, I was the youngest in the squad.

The picture below is the full Fighter and Observer Squadrons at Stretton. That's me sitting on the ground, 3 in on the left, holding a cup which I had been awarded for an aerobatic display.

This photograph shows part of a page from one of my early Logbooks when I was flying my first aircraft, the Percival Prentice aircraft at Syerston.

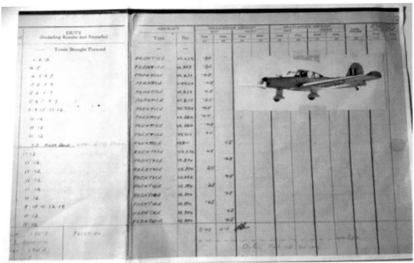

On finishing my training course at Syerston I received this Flying Assessment

HstT774 WL8943-P.103 20,000(2) 5.51 Gp.840 F. & C. Ltd., London R.A.F. FORM 414A

COURSE ENDING

SUMMARY of FLYING and ASSESSMENTS FOR YEAR COMMENCING 1st 14 th MAY 1954
[*For Officer, insert "FEBRUARY"; For Airman Pilot, insert "AUGUST."]

| | S.E. AIRCRAFT | | M.E. AIRCRAFT | | TOTAL for year | GRAND TOTAL |
	Day	Night	Day	Night	for the year	All Service Flying
DUAL	83·30	7·50	—	—	91·20	92·20
PILOT	84·30	8·20	—	—	92·50	92·50
PASSENGER	—	—	—	—		

ASSESSMENT of ABILITY (To be assessed as :—Exceptional, Above the Average, Average, Below Average)

(i) AS A Pupil †PILOT ABOVE THE AVERAGE

(ii) AS PILOT-NAVIGATOR/NAVIGATOR EXCEPTIONAL.

(iii) IN BOMBING N·A

(iv) IN AIR GUNNERY N·A

(v) IN INSTRUMENT FLYING WHITE RATING. STANDARD
† Insert :—"F.", "C.B.", "G.R.", "F.B.", "Instructor", etc.

ANY POINTS IN FLYING OR AIRMANSHIP WHICH SHOULD BE WATCHED

NIL

Signature .... WG.CDR.

Date 14 TH MAY 1954. Officer Commanding No.22 F.T.S. R.A.F. SYERSTON.

It was a proud day for me on 14th May 1954 when I received my certificate and my Naval Pilots Flying Badge, I was aged 19.

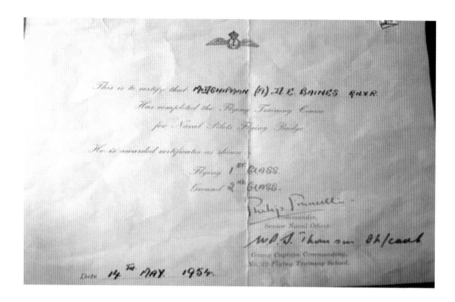

This portrait picture of me was taken when I had joined B.E.A. and was on a stop-over in Belfast. In the Navy aviators' wings are worn on the left sleeve but in commercial airlines, as in the R.A.F., the wings are worn on the left breast of a uniform.

My wedding day 24th May 1960

My beautiful wife Barbara and myself on the right with my brother
Ralph and his wife Joan on the left, attending a formal dinner.

I got to meet many interesting people on the flights that I Captained, the Crown Prince Akihito and Princess Michiko were extremely friendly and gracious. They are now the Emperor and Empress of Japan.

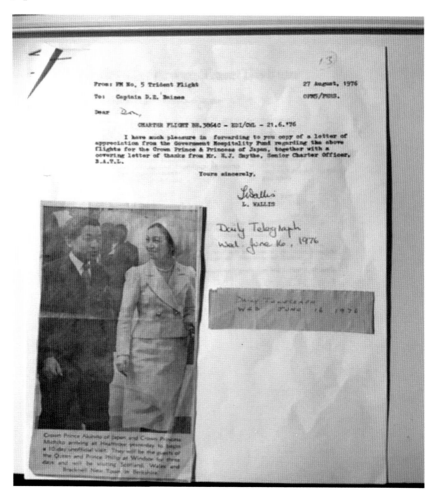

My story tells of the gift that I received from them, the silver cufflinks shaped as aeroplanes which I have worn on so many occasions.

Just a few of the many letters and memos which I was very pleased
to receive.

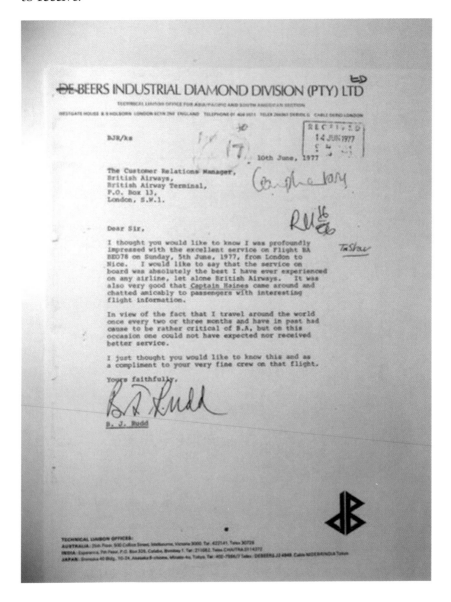

DE BEERS INDUSTRIAL DIAMOND DIVISION (PTY) LTD

BJR/ks

10th June, 1977

The Customer Relations Manager,
British Airways,
British Airway Terminal,
P.O. Box 13,
London, S.W.1.

Dear Sir,

I thought you would like to know I was profoundly
impressed with the excellent service on Flight BA
BE078 on Sunday, 5th June, 1977, from London to
Nice. I would like to say that the service on
board was absolutely the best I have ever experienced
on any airline, let alone British Airways. It was
also very good that Captain Haines came around and
chatted amicably to passengers with interesting
flight information.

In view of the fact that I travel around the world
once every two or three months and have in past had
cause to be rather critical of B.A, but on this
occasion one could not have expected nor received
better service.

I just thought you would like to know this and as
a compliment to your very fine crew on that flight.

Yours faithfully,

B. J. Rudd

It was good to know that passengers' appreciation was passed on to
Captains and the crews.

V - copy to Cpr Baines psc. — *for our info.*

FROM Adviser Future Aircraft   *16*   1179

TO   : Flight Crew Manager TriStar/DC10   23rd August 1977

RE 007 PARIS/LONDON-18 AUGUST

Because of ATC problems this flight was some five hours delayed. I would
like to commend the action of Captain Baines, in speaking to the passengers
in the lounge on two occasions, and explaining to them to the best of his
knowledge what the situation was and what was likely to transpire. The effect
of their depressed and disgruntled attitude was little short of miraculous .

I imagine that many others of your flight crew will have been acting as effectively
but it was only flight 007 that I had the opportunity of observing at first hand.

R H WHITBY

It has always given me great pleasure to be able to explain to people how safe it is flying in aircraft and what a wonderful experience it is. I do recall settling the nerves of many passengers over the years when I was flying.

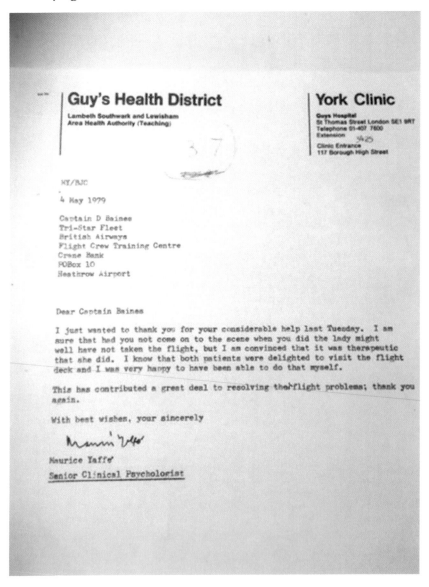

Guy's Health District

Lambeth Southwark and Lewisham
Area Health Authority (Teaching)

York Clinic

Guys Hospital
St Thomas Street London SE1 9RT
Telephone 01-407 7600
Extension   425
Clinic Entrance
117 Borough High Street

MY/BJC

4 May 1979

Captain D Baines
Tri-Star Fleet
British Airways
Flight Crew Training Centre
Crane Bank
POBox 10
Heathrow Airport

Dear Captain Baines

I just wanted to thank you for your considerable help last Tuesday. I am sure that had you not come on to the scene when you did the lady might well have not taken the flight, but I am convinced that it was therapeutic that she did. I know that both patients were delighted to visit the flight deck and I was very happy to have been able to do that myself.

This has contributed a great deal to resolving the flight problems; thank you again.

With best wishes, your sincerely

Maurice Yaffe
Senior Clinical Psychologist

It is very much appreciated when people take the time to write their thanks, which are always gratefully received.

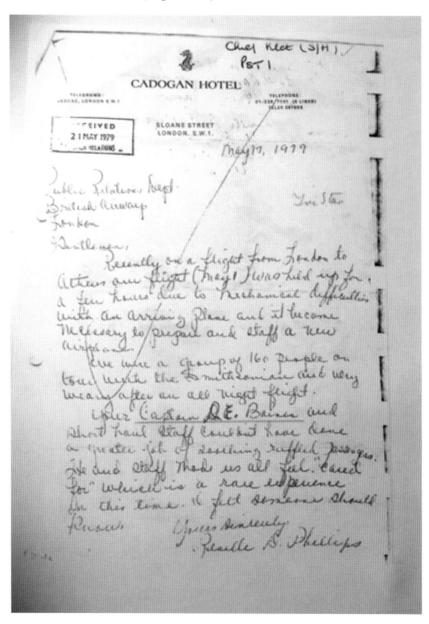

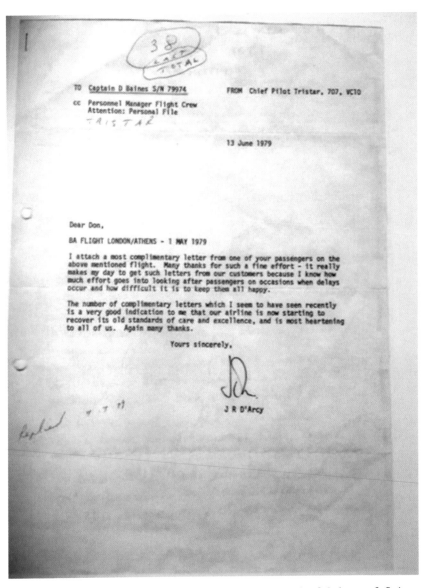

TO Captain D Baines S/N 79974   FROM Chief Pilot Tristar, 707, VC10

cc Personnel Manager Flight Crew
    Attention: Personal File

    TRISTAR

                                      13 June 1979

Dear Don,

BA FLIGHT LONDON/ATHENS - 1 MAY 1979

I attach a most complimentary letter from one of your passengers on the
above mentioned flight. Many thanks for such a fine effort - it really
makes my day to get such letters from our customers because I know how
much effort goes into looking after passengers on occasions when delays
occur and how difficult it is to keep them all happy.

The number of complimentary letters which I seem to have seen recently
is a very good indication to me that our airline is now starting to
recover its old standards of care and excellence, and is most heartening
to all of us. Again many thanks.

                Yours sincerely,

                J R D'Arcy

These letters bring back to my memory my wonderful days of flying.

As do my small collection of model aeroplanes, all of which are planes that I have personally flown.

My favourite aeroplane being the Seafury FB2 Fighter Bomber

It is true to say that I always thoroughly enjoyed flying all the aircraft.

Below is the Viscount 800 which I flew when first appointed as a BA Captain.

The Trident 3 shown here is the plane I was given to fly when moving down from Manchester to London.

Another wonderful aeroplane that I enjoyed was the Tristar Lockheed 1011.

This was the plane in which I undertook the Blind Landing at Orly Airport.

Life carried on after the news that I could no longer fly aircrafts. My wonderful wife Barbara and I enjoyed attending the many weddings of our nieces and nephews as well as those of the children of our friends.

Regrettably due to Covid restrictions my wife Barbara's funeral was a small occasion with only 8 people allowed to attend. In her memory I wore my BA airline uniform, as she used to say to me – she loved her man in uniform.

Barbara would be the first person to tell me that "Life goes on" and so to finish on a positive theme I close with a picture of myself together with my good friend Dennis Woods (sitting left) visiting the Trident 3 aircraft in the Air Sciences Museum at Farnborough Airport. Also in the Cockpit is Retired Captain David Warren who assists at the Museum. I can certainly recommend it as a well worthwhile place to visit — fascinating and I look forward to taking my grandsons when they are next able to visit me from South Africa.

Such Happy Memories ....